CELEBRATING ELEPHANTS

Celebrating Elephants

Walter the Educator

Silent King Books

SILENT KING BOOKS

SKB

First Printing, 2024

dedicated to those who love collecting elephant artifacts

ELEPHANTS

In ancient lands where earth's embrace

Celebrating Elephants

Meets sky with velvet hue,

Celebrating Elephants

Roam giants draped in wisdom's grace,

Celebrating Elephants

With grandeur through and through.

Celebrating Elephants

Their shadows stretch across the plain,

Celebrating Elephants

Beneath the sun's gold eye,

Celebrating Elephants

With tusks like ivory lightning's gain,

Celebrating Elephants

They pierce the morning sky.

Celebrating Elephants

The forest whispers sacred tales

Celebrating Elephants

Of ancestors long gone,

Celebrating Elephants

Where elephantine trails prevail,

Celebrating Elephants

A timeless, ancient song.

Celebrating Elephants

Majestic matriarchs lead forth,

Celebrating Elephants

Their kin in careful line,

Celebrating Elephants

With steps that mark the sacred earth,

Celebrating Elephants

A legacy divine.

Celebrating Elephants

The elephants, in silent might,

Celebrating Elephants

With skin like weathered stone,

Celebrating Elephants

Hold stories in their soulful sight,

Celebrating Elephants

Of times the world has known.

Celebrating Elephants

With trunks that sway like ancient trees,

Celebrating Elephants

They touch the heavens' rim,

Celebrating Elephants

And trumpet calls that ride the breeze

Celebrating Elephants

Are nature's primal hymn.

Celebrating Elephants

In rivers deep and jungles dense,

Celebrating Elephants

They journey, bold and free,

Celebrating Elephants

Their presence speaks of recompense,

Celebrating Elephants

Of nature's wild decree.

Celebrating Elephants

The moonlight dances on their backs,

Celebrating Elephants

A silver-shaded dream,

Celebrating Elephants

As night's soft whispers, velvet blacks,

Celebrating Elephants

Enfold them in a gleam.

Celebrating Elephants

Each wrinkle on their sturdy hide

Celebrating Elephants

Is like a script unfurled,

Celebrating Elephants

A tale of how the earth did bide

Celebrating Elephants

Through ages in this world.

Celebrating Elephants

Their ears, wide fans that catch the breeze,

Celebrating Elephants

Are maps of winds and storms,

Celebrating Elephants

Of desert whispers, ocean pleas,

Celebrating Elephants

Of countless weathered forms.

Celebrating Elephants

The elephants, in silence speak,

Celebrating Elephants

In ways the heart can feel,

Celebrating Elephants

Of strength in moments seeming meek,

Celebrating Elephants

Of scars that slowly heal.

Celebrating Elephants

ABOUT THE CREATOR

Walter the Educator is one of the pseudonyms for Walter Anderson. Formally educated in Chemistry, Business, and Education, he is an educator, an author, a diverse entrepreneur, and he is the son of a disabled war veteran. "Walter the Educator" shares his time between educating and creating. He holds interests and owns several creative projects that entertain, enlighten, enhance, and educate, hoping to inspire and motivate you.

Follow, find new works, and stay up to date
with Walter the Educator™
at WaltertheEducator.com

Milton Keynes UK
Ingram Content Group UK Ltd.
UKHW050858210624
444436UK00014B/267

9 798330 229826